Introducing
Māori
culture

Don Stafford

RAUPO

ACKNOWLEDGEMENTS

A vital element in any work such as this must be a close association with recognised experts in various fields. A lifetime
which has included friendships with many knowledgeable
elders of Te Arawa tribe has been of immense benefit. I have
also been extremely fortunate to have had the complete
cooperation of the director and staff of the New Zealand
Maori Arts and Crafts Institute. A long association there with
Clive Fugill and Emily Schuster, renowned respectively in the
fields of carving and weaving, has allowed me to enquire into
various facets of 'things Maori' not otherwise readily available.
My friend the late Kuru Waretini and his successor Arihia
Carrington have both given me ready access to material held
by the Institute and this, together with the overall approval
and support of the former director, John Marsh, has made the
task much easier than would normally have been the case.

I am similarly indebted to John Perry, former director of the
Rotorua Museum of Art and History, and his staff, who have
always made their facilities freely available to me. Their
remarkable collection of historic photographs has been of
particular value, and their consistent support and concern for
my needs is deeply appreciated. My gratitude must also go to
all at Rotorua's public library, where every possible assistance
and courtesy has always been provided.

Holger Leue

A RAUPO BOOK
Published by the Penguin Group
Penguin Group (NZ), 67 Apollo Drive, Rosedale,
North Shore 0632, New Zealand (a division of Pearson New Zealand Ltd)

Penguin Books Ltd, Registered Offices: 80 Strand, London, WC2R 0RL, England

Originally published by Reed Publishing (NZ) Ltd as *Tangata Whenua*, 1996
First published as *Introducing Maori Culture*, 1997
Reprinted 1999, 2000, 2001, 2002, 2003, 2004, 2005, 2006, 2007

First published by Penguin Group (NZ), 2008
1 3 5 7 9 10 8 6 4 2

ISBN: 978 0 14 301082 1

A catalogue record for this book is available
from the National Library of New Zealand.

www.penguin.co.nz

Contents

Introduction

There is a growing awareness among most New Zealanders that they are now part of a distinctly bicultural community. Such a realisation has brought with it a need for material that will stimulate and foster a greater understanding of this unique heritage.

The demand is generally for a brief, easily understood but authoritative account of the background of our indigenous Polynesians, the New Zealand Maori. Such an interest demands an explanation of their origins, their vast migrations, their arrival in this country and their development here both in pre- and post-European times.

The content of this book is intended to meet these requirements and offer an easily absorbed but comprehensive coverage of 'things Maori'. A wide diversity of topics is covered, with information drawn from tradition, myth and history. It will answer most questions commonly asked about the original human occupants of Aotearoa.

Pronunciation

Thirteen letters and two digraphs make up the Maori alphabet. The letters are a, e, h, i, k, m, n, o, p, r, t, u, w, and the digraphs ng and wh. In general, it is only the vowels and perhaps the digraphs that provide a problem for non-Maori speakers.

Pronunciation of the vowels is as follows: 'a' as the u in putty; 'e' as the e in pet; 'i' as the ee in sheep; 'o' as the o in port; 'u' as the u in rule. Though no two consonants (other than the digraphs) ever occur together, vowels frequently do. Where this occurs, pronunciation remains the same but is simply doubled in value. All syllables and words end with a vowel.

The digraph 'ng' is pronounced as the ng in singer. The 'wh', though generally given the f sound as in fetch should, in fact, be softer, as in when or where (or the ph in epitaph).

Glossary

ariki . . . . tribal leader

aruhe . . . . edible fern-root

atua . . . . god/supernatural being

haka . . . . posture dance

hangi . . . . earth oven/food from

hapu . . . . subtribe within iwi

harakeke . . . . flax (*Phormium tenax*)

Hauhau . . . . anti-British cult

hongi . . . . greet, press noses

hue . . . . cultivated gourd

huia . . . . extinct bird

iwi . . . . distinct tribal group

kahu huruhuru . . . . feathered cloak

kahu kuri . . . . dogskin cloak

kainga . . . . house/settlement

kakareao . . . . supplejack
(*Rhipogonum scandens*)

karaka . . . . species of tree
(*Corynocarpus laevigata*)

karanga . . . . call/summon

kauri . . . . species of tree
(*Agathis australis*)

kete . . . . kit/basket

kohanga reo . . . . language nest

kokowai . . . . natural earth/oil paint

korowai . . . . woven cloak

kumara . . . . sweet potato

kura kaupapa Maori . . . Maori-speaking school

maihi . . . . frontal barge boards of
house

manuhiri . . . . visitor

marae . . . . village plaza

moko . . . . tattoo

pa . . . . fortified village

pataka . . . . storage building on piles

patua . . . . bark container

pingao . . . . coastal grass

piupiu . . . . decorative skirt

poi . . . . ball on string/dancing aid

pounamu . . . . greenstone (jade)

puhi . . . . virgin/high-born maiden

rangatira . . . . chief/aristocrat

raupo . . . . bullrush

rourou . . . . woven platter

rua . . . . storage pit

rua poka . . . . excavated storage cave

tangata whenua . . . . . . local inhabitant

tangihanga . . . . mourning/funeral

taniko . . . . fine decorative weave

tapu . . . . prohibition/sacred

taro . . . . root crop

taurekareka . . . . slave

ti kouka . . . . cabbage tree
(*Cordyline australis*)

ti rakau . . . . game/amusement

ti ringa . . . . game/amusement

toetoe . . . . species of plant
(*Arundo conspicua*)

tohunga . . . . priest/expert

toiki . . . . loosely woven kit

totara . . . . species of tree
(*Podocarpus totara*)

umu . . . . earth oven

waiata . . . . song

ware . . . . commoner

wero . . . . challenge to visitors

whakapapa . . . . genealogy

whanau . . . . family
(immediate and extended)

wharekai . . . . dining place

whare kohanga . . . . . . nest house/birthplace

whare wananga . . . . . . place of learning

whariki . . . . floor mat

wiwi . . . . coarse grass/rushes

Origins and migrations

Human occupation of the area we think of as Polynesia, Micronesia and Melanesia was by a people of Southeast Asian origin. The movement began perhaps as many as 50,000 years ago or more and during the following centuries resulted in the occupation of Australia, Tasmania and New Guinea which at some period were joined to form a single continent. The rising sea levels (past ice age) eventually isolated the people into separate groups allowing them to develop distinct cultural assemblages.

At a period between 4,000 and 6,000 years ago, these people were poised in Near Oceania (which includes New Guinea, the islands of the Bismarck Archipelago and the Solomons) ready for their great move eastwards. By 1200 BC the migrants had arrived in Tonga and by 1000 BC in Samoa. It was in those two islands that the people probably became the first true Polynesians and they are recognisable as such from the archaeological records and other studies.

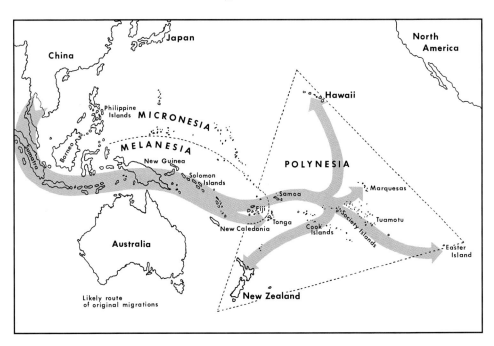

Holger Leue

The migrations continued and probably by the time of the birth of Christ the islands to the east, such as the Society Islands, the Marquesas and probably the Tuamotus, had been reached. A long period of isolation then seems to have followed, long enough to enable distinct differences to appear between these people and their parent group to the west. These differences in culture and language still distinguish the western from the eastern Polynesians.

New Zealand, with its cool-temperate climate, rugged coastline and broken terrain, presented a serious challenge to the first Polynesian arrivals.

Other CONTACTS

There is little doubt that at some stage before the arrival of Europeans in the Pacific there was contact between Polynesians and Micronesians, and between Polynesians and South American Indians — but neither group contributed in any great degree to the world of Polynesia.

Further migrations meant that by AD 500 Rapanui (Easter Island) was also occupied. Before the end of the seventh century Hawaii had received its first settlers and before another 300 years had passed the Polynesians may have arrived in Aotearoa.

7

Pacific peoples

The three major peoples within the Pacific consist of Micronesians, Melanesians and Polynesians. The world of Polynesia lies within a vast triangle stretching from Hawaii in the north, to New Zealand in the south and Easter Island in the east. To the west of Polynesia lies Melanesia and to the northwest, Micronesia.

It was with the journeys of Captain Cook that attention was drawn in a major way to the differences between peoples and cultures in various parts of the Pacific Ocean. The young naturalist, George Forster, who accompanied Cook on his second voyage of 1772–75, was one of the first to comment on the obvious physical differences between Polynesians and Melanesians. He described Polynesians as tall, athletic, light coloured and of benevolent temperament.

Later observers noticed that in contrast to Melanesians, the Polynesians had hair that was usually straight to wavy (not woolly) and they often showed a Mongoloid affinity, having a scarcity of body hair and an Asian-type of eye form. However, contact with Europeans (in particular) during the past 200 years has produced considerable diversity among all major Polynesian groups.

Eunice of Efate Island, Vanuatu (above left) is Melanesian, and Taima of Te Whakarewarewa, Rotorua (right) is Polynesian.

POLYNESIANS

There seems little doubt that the origins of the Polynesians are to be found in Southeast Asia. There is, however, considerable diversity of opinion as to whether they left that area and passed through Melanesia as Polynesians or whether their distinctive traits only developed after they reached the area now defined as Polynesia. In their own traditions the New Zealand Polynesians, the Maori, speak of a nebulous homeland, Hawaiki, as their place of origin and upon death, the spirit returns to this place, thought of as being somewhere to the west.

Apart from the indigenous Maori, Polynesians from many parts of the Pacific now make their permanent home here in Aotearoa/New Zealand, which has by far the largest Polynesian population of any nation.

A Polynesian Cook Islander dances to Malaysian drummers.

Gil Hanly

9

Voyages and vessels

The ability of a people to travel across water presupposes a marine technology. A west to east movement from the larger islands through Melanesia and on to the smaller volcanic islands of Polynesia required greater skill than the movements within Melanesia itself. Similarly the much greater stretches of open water encountered in central and eastern Polynesia called for a more elaborate and suitable type of vessel. The ability to cope with these demands also presumes a development of the skills of sailing and navigation so often attributed to the Polynesians.

The first people to move south from the Southeast Asian or Indonesian mainland, perhaps more than 50,000 years ago, would have needed little more than a convenient log or raft to cross the narrow stretches of water remaining when the sea was at its lowest point. However, by the time Polynesians were first encountered by Europeans, their vessels ranged from simple dugouts, to single outrigger, to great double-hulled vessels and the magnificent and highly adorned war canoes of New Zealand.

There is little doubt that it was the great double-hulled Polynesian canoes that ultimately brought the Maori to

Top left: A portrait of Captain James Cook by John Webber.

Left: In their giant double-hulled canoes the Polynesian peoples ranged as far as Hawaii in the north, Easter Island in the east, and New Zealand in the south.

that canoes were vital to the Maori, though not simply as a means of transport. Their finest vessels — their war canoes — were sometimes 30 m in length and capable of carrying a hundred or more paddlers. They also possessed an element of spirituality, of mana and prestige, to those who owned or sailed in them.

The arrival of the Polynesian people in New Zealand was the final step in a series of remarkable voyages which saw them touch every spot of land, however remote, throughout the entire South Pacific and provide a colony for every habitable island and atoll, earning them the title of 'Vikings of the Sunrise'.

Aotearoa. Similar, though perhaps smaller, vessels were still in use here when Captain Cook arrived.

Return VOYAGES

There is scant evidence (other than from traditional sources) that voyaging between New Zealand and the Polynesian homelands to the north took place once this country had been settled. An absence of return voyages may have been the result of a radical change in canoe design. The superb forests and great trees available in New Zealand undoubtedly allowed for the ultimate development of vessels which, though not suited to long ocean voyages are, many believe, the pinnacle of Maori artistry and design.

With a marine background second to none, a world of ocean around them and vast inland waterways it is natural

Top left: The giant New Zealand kauri, exploited early by the British Navy for ship's masts and spars.

Above: Monuments mark landing places of migrant canoes arriving from Hawaiki about AD 1350. This monument stands at Maketu (Bay of Plenty), the arrival point of Te Arawa canoe.

Islands of Maui

Holger Leue

Unique to New Zealand, the tuatara is the only surviving representative of an order of reptiles which became extinct throughout Asia, Africa, Europe and North America more than 100 million years ago.

Geologically speaking the islands of Polynesia are of recent origin with the exception of New Zealand, which has a past going back millions of years. Long isolation has allowed it to develop without outside influence. And yet some of its more unusual inhabitants such as the moa (a giant flightless bird) and the tuatara (the sole survivor of a group of ancient relatives of the extinct dinosaurs) are part of a continental heritage indicating that New Zealand was once joined to a larger land mass, perhaps part of a vast southern continent that included Australia and its surrounding islands.

Polynesians, however, have legends which tell a different story, one that concerns an ancient demi-god known as Maui-tikitiki-a-Taranga.

Maui's mother was Taranga, who already had four sons when Maui was born. He was a weakling at birth and in disgust Taranga tossed him into the sea wrapped only in the top-knot from her hair. Tangaroa, god of the sea, was touched by this piteous little object so he cradled the child in a nest of seaweed and nurtured him carefully until he developed into a fine child. Eventually Tangaroa cast Maui gently back upon the beach near where his mother lived. Taranga found her child, was overjoyed and at once accepted him back into her family, giving him the name Maui-tikitiki-a-Taranga because he had been wrapped in the top-knot from her hair.

Exploits of MAUI

The adventures of Maui would fill a book and throughout Polynesia he is credited with providing most of those things that are indispensable to all of us, even today.

Through skill and perseverance he discovered fire and how it might be kindled and controlled. It was only because he travelled far to the east and snared the sun with a great net and beat him unmercifully that our day is as long as it is. Before this time the sun rushed across the sky in a matter of moments.

A fisherman of renown, Maui dragged up from the depths of the ocean wondrous fish which, once caught, became firm land. In this way Te Ika a Maui (the North Island of New Zealand), Tonga, Rakahanga (in the northern Cook Islands), Hawaii and other big fish were hauled to the surface and fixed in the positions they now occupy.

Master carver Tuti Tukaokao, with 'Maui capturing the Sun'.

Jack Lang

13

The discovery

Experts now suggest that the islands of New Zealand were first occupied at least by the thirteenth century, perhaps earlier, and that its first immigrants came from central Polynesia. Maori legends support this with stories concerning Rangiatea (Raiatea in the Society Islands) and Rarotonga (in the Cook Islands). It is also now generally believed that this country was probably settled only once in a major way. There may have been occasional subsequent arrivals but all were from the same original source.

The Maori people themselves almost universally claim descent from one or other of a number of named canoes (referred to figuratively as 'The Fleet') supposed to have arrived here between the thirteenth and sixteenth centuries. Whatever the case, it is reliably held that these first settlers were all of the same Polynesian stock and remained so at least until the advent of the European.

Over the years a number of terms, including Moriori and Maruiwi, have been coined to distinguish the earliest wave of immigrants, said to have been supplanted by the later 'Fleet' arrivals. Such terms and theories have long since been discarded with the exception of Moriori, the name used today to indicate original Chatham Island settlers.

Rotorua Museum of Art & History

Holger Leue

The innumerable waterways of New Zealand made canoes a vital form of transport for the Maori. They were quick to take advantage of fabric sails in early post-European times.

White Island in the Bay of Plenty was one of several active volcanic sites noted by the early Maori and recorded in legend.

Kupe the EXPLORER

The discovery of Aotearoa, according to some Maori tradition, was first made by the legendary Polynesian explorer Kupe. He lived on the island of Raiatea, spoken of in legends as Hawaiki. Kupe and his companion Ngahue set out in two canoes known as *Matahorua* and *Tawiri-rangi* and sailed south to see what lay beyond the horizon. Eventually the canoes reached this country which, from the sea, resembled a white cloud in the distance. Kupe's wife, Hine-te-aparangi, called out: 'He ao, he ao!' (a cloud, a cloud!') and so the place was named Aotea – bright cloud. In time that name became Aotearoa, now commonly known as 'The Land of the Long White Cloud'.

Kupe and his fellow travellers had many adventures while circumnavigating the North and South Islands of Aotearoa; in the South Island at Arahura they discovered pounamu (greenstone), and nearby at Wairere they killed a giant flightless bird, the moa. Both greenstone and the preserved flesh of the moa were taken back to Hawaiki as examples of some of the treasures to be found in this new land.

The story of this remarkable voyage of discovery was told and retold to succeeding generations. When disputes and warfare erupted in Hawaiki during the fourteenth century, the disaffected groups decided to leave their homeland forever and travel south to occupy the land discovered by their ancestor Kupe.

The giant flightless moa now exists only in the fossil record. This depiction of the moa was painted by Paul Martinson.

Survival

The breadfruit (left) and coconut (above) are staple foods further north, but will not grow in New Zealand's temperate climate.

Once in New Zealand the Polynesians had to make a fundamental change to their lifestyle if they were to survive and prosper. In particular they had to adjust to an almost totally new food supply.

Imported FOODS

Because this new land was entirely within the temperate zone none of their previous traditional crops grew here. From the exhaustive list of tropical foodstuffs (most of which they presumably brought with them), few except the kumara (sweet potato), hue (gourd), taro and yam seem to have survived. Only the kumara provided a valuable crop, though it was labour intensive, strictly seasonal

and difficult to store. The hue could, in certain places, be grown with great care; taro survived only in a very few favoured areas while the yam seems barely to have existed.

Native SUPPLIES

There was, however, no immediate danger of starvation. The coastal waters teemed with fish, shellfish, crayfish, crabs and other seafood. The inland rivers and lakes carried many freshwater species and in most areas eels (and sometimes lamprey) could be taken in vast numbers.

New Zealand forests provided none of the constant supplies the immigrants had known in their homelands. However, a range of edible plants and berries were gradually discovered. Fruit of the karaka and tawa trees provided abundant crops, though each required special preparation and cooking to rid them of poison. The ti kouka (cabbage tree) was also important. Once known as the palm lily but now classified with agaves, its huge rhizome and tender palm heads were a valued food source. Probably the single most important edible plant was the rarauhe (common bracken fern), its rhizome providing a greater food supply than all other cultivated plants put together.

The forest birds provided a source of succulent flesh. Birds in New Zealand were particularly vulnerable. Free (as they had always been) from any predator, many had become ground foragers. The two most widely known of these were the moa, some species standing 3 m high, and the smaller kiwi. Trapped in a variety of ways, birds were often preserved in their own fat for future use. The new settlers also brought with them the dog and the rat — the first non-human predators. Both were valued as a source of flesh until well into the nineteenth century.

Above: Originating in South America, the kumara was introduced into New Zealand and became an important cultivated food plant.

Left: This massive coastal midden, made up of the remains of shellfish consumed by Maori, indicates the importance of this food.

Strict CONTROL

Matters affecting cultivation, fishing or hunting were governed strictly by experts, who supervised collective efforts or laid down rigid rules for individual action. Carefully preserved calendars based on phases of the moon were adhered to, and conservation was a determining factor in the taking of natural resources. There was a dramatic change with the introduction of European food plants. Of these the potato was by far the most important but hardly less valued was the pig, first released here by Captain Cook in 1769.

Above: The rhizome of the common bracken fern (rarauhe) provided a constant and abundant food source almost everywhere.

Left: The cabbage tree (ti kouka).

PREPARATION

Apart from roasting over an open fire, food was, as in most of Polynesia, cooked in an umu (earth oven). A hole was dug in the ground into which heated stones were placed, water being added to create steam. The food, wrapped in leaves, was laid on the stones and the hole covered with earth. This form of preparation is still favoured throughout New Zealand, particularly at Maori functions.

Both the oven and its food content are generally referred to today as hangi. Apart from having traditional importance to the Maori, this has, with some refinements, become a significant feature within the visitor industry wherever there is Maori participation.

Above: Hangi in thermal area.

Below: Cultivations close at hand and further afield were a vital part of daily existence wherever settlements were established.

19

Settlement

The much lower temperatures in New Zealand demanded a different system of housing for its first immigrants from Polynesia. There was a need for protection against the colder evenings, especially during the winter.

Above: Elaborate storehouses were constructed to hold taonga (treasures).

Above: Where possible, caves were dug as storage places. Some bore names. This cave at Pukurahi Pa, Lake Rotoiti was called Parangiakaikore.

HOUSES

Even where family housing was of a permanent nature, dwellings were invariably of one room. They served only as sleeping quarters or shelters against the worst weather conditions. Usually a few hearth stones allowed a small fire to be maintained for warmth. Food was never permitted within these quarters and all cooking took place outside, sometimes under temporary shelter.

Ordinary dwellings were generally rectangular, varying from 3 m to 5 m in length and 2 m to 3 m in width. As a rule they were sunk into the ground as a form of insulation and were either with or without walls. The frame was of light pole construction and packed with tightly bundled grass, wiwi (reed) or raupo (bullrush). Where walls existed they were sometimes constructed of close-set trunks of tree ferns while roofs were thatched or covered with bark of the totara tree. Some settlements had larger houses, perhaps 9 m or 10 m in length. These probably belonged to chiefs and would also serve as places of assembly for the local community and as accommodation for guests.

Food STORAGE

Food storage facilities were of vital importance and existed in each community. The most common were rua (pits dug in the ground), rua poka (cave-like excavations where suitable rock existed), and pataka (roofed-over house-like

European architecture with native building materials.

excavations or elevated buildings). The latter were sometimes of great tribal prestige, the more elaborate often used to store tribal treasures rather than food.

Superior BUILDINGS

Few ordinary buildings would have featured carvings in pre-European times. Each village would, however, strive to provide at least its meeting house and pataka (if it had one) with some ornamentation. It was a matter of prestige and tribute to the building, the size, quality and number of carvings depending on the economic strength of the inhabitants.

New METHODS

The arrival of Europeans brought a rapid change to Maori building methods and materials. Steel axes and saws in particular, the skills of pit sawing, shingle splitting and the use of joinery replaced traditional tools and systems. Where early traders or missionaries were active these changes were soon apparent. In more remote areas traditional methods persisted until the mid-nineteenth century.

These new tools and skills meant that important buildings could be made much larger. A gradual cessation of intertribal warfare and more stable communities encouraged this development. Carvings, both exterior and interior, became a feature of a number of these buildings, some of which are preserved today as national treasures.

Individual houses of weatherboard and shingle roof became common, though still generally of one room. With these, however, came a change of traditional attitude that saw external chimneys and a fireplace with cooking facilities in a living area. For the first time local stone (where available) was quarried to provide these. In some areas, chiefs of importance built larger houses of several rooms, often of European design.

The marae

Of greatest significance within any Maori community is the marae, or plaza, together with its associated wharenui (meeting house) and wharekai (dining room). The dining room today replaces the earlier pataka, or storehouse, and is where food is eaten communally once formal matters have taken their course on the marae. The marae and meeting house are virtually insep-arable and together create the venue where everything of tribal consequence is conducted. This is where local protocol is of paramount concern and an insight into Maori custom can best be observed.

In most centres the marae bears its own significant name. The meeting house invariably does and the name is generally that of a revered male ancestor whose wife provides a name for the adjacent dining room.

The meeting house is believed to have a prestige and spiritual identity of its own. It represents, in fact, the ancestor himself, its maihi (frontal barge boards) portraying his welcoming arms, the

At this major gathering the tribal elders are seated across the front of the whare tupuna, with the men of the tribe standing behind them, and the women ready to greet the manuhiri (visitors) in front.

Jack Lang

22

rafters his ribs, and the ridge-pole his spine. It is for this reason that such houses are referred to as whare tupuna (ancestor house).

Where carvings adorn the house they provide not only a distinctive beauty but a record of ancestry and history. However, the features within each carving (with few exceptions) are identifiable only to those with a thorough knowledge of local tribal traditions.

The formal WELCOME

On the marae, a powhiri or formal welcome is a moving experience. The tangata whenua (host people) and manuhiri (visitors) both have strict and traditional roles to play.

In general, visitors always wait beyond the marae entrance until a karanga (a specific call to enter) is given. Led by the women, the visitors then move slowly across the marae towards the meeting house, stopping some distance in front. There is a pause for a brief period of mourning, a time to remember the departed of both groups, their grief often expressed by prolonged crying from the women of both sides.

The visitors then move to one side and are seated, the men of the party (who will probably speak to the assembly) occupying at least the front row. Formal speeches begin and once concluded the visitors move forward to greet their hosts with a handshake and hongi — the pressing of noses.

When a particularly important visitor arrives, a challenge, known as the wero, may be offered. This reflects an ancient ceremony where visitors are required to indicate whether they approach with a desire for peace or war.

An initial call from a sentry alerts the tangata whenua of the approach of a

Above: Powhiri (formal welcome) Women dressed in traditional black welcome guests onto the marae. The party of visitors responds to the greeting, and individuals are welcomed with the hongi (pressing of noses).

Interior of the whare tupuna at Waitangi, Northland.

Jack Lang

party. Then a challenging warrior, armed with a taiaha (long club), darts out towards the visitors, placing some small object on the ground in front of them. He taunts them with war-like gestures and exhibits his skill with the weapon. There is a pause before the visiting leader picks up the object, signifying peaceful intentions. At that point the challenging warrior turns back and leads the party onto the marae.

Carving styles
Below:
The highly decorated interior of a Te Arawa meeting house, (left) contrasts with the plain exterior of a nineteenth century house (whare).

The land

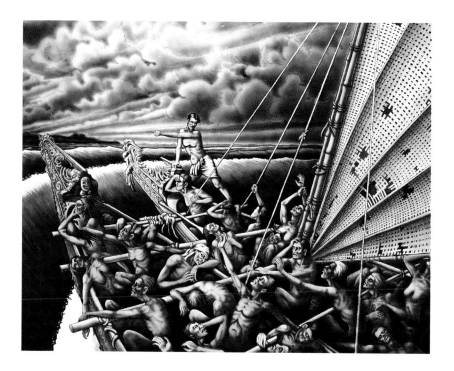

OCCUPATION

The traditional 'Fleet' canoes made their landfalls at various points around the coastline. The respective crews and passengers first claimed and settled those immediate areas then moved inland. The country was eventually divided up into distinct territories, each largely inhabited by those claiming descent from the occupants of one or other of the canoes. In general, these major subdivisions have remained static since that time though some boundaries have altered with the fortunes of the original occupiers.

After a dangerous and difficult journey, the traditional 'Fleet' canoes make their landfall in Aotearoa.

SUBDIVISION

As populations expanded, subtribes of each major group came into being. These in time separated into even smaller units, each autonomous and occupying an area over which it claimed authority. Inevitably, conflict arose between various groups, generally over territorial rights. However, a united front was generally shown when aggression from outside threatened, or when aggression against an outside foe seemed justified and was decided upon.

Ownership RIGHTS

Land tenure within tribal areas was based on inheritance through ancestors or conquest. Recognised chiefs were often able to claim favoured areas because of their prestige and authority. Smaller groups and families held no specific title but were recognised as legitimate occupiers by their contemporaries. They were also able to pass on these rights to successive generations. Rules of inheritance were numerous, however, and not all descendants held succession rights. Many productive cultivations were occupied and worked communally; the title was obviously considered a tribal one.

Treaty of WAITANGI

European land tenure laws brought great confusion to the Maori. Before 1840 sales of leases and land to Europeans were arranged by private treaty. This led to many misunderstandings and disputes. The Treaty of Waitangi, an agreement between the chiefs of New Zealand and the Queen of England, was in part intended to remedy this situation. Under its provisions all purchases of land were supposed to have been through the Crown, acting as agent for the Maori. The terms of the Treaty required the Maori to cede the sovereignty of New Zealand to the Queen. In return, she would guarantee them

The Waikato copy of the Treaty of Waitangi, now held in the National Archives, Wellington.

continued and undisputed possession of their lands.

Despite the admirable intentions, observance of Treaty obligations has been often ignored. Misunderstandings and disputes over land have never been extinguished. A government act of 1865, abolishing the Crown's pre-emptive rights and allowing direct land purchases by Europeans from individual Maori, compounded these problems. The resulting despair and mistrust of some tribes led to the Land Wars of the 1860s and early 1870s. Confiscation of large territories from Maori who had taken up arms against the Government created resentment that still exists today.

Recent years have seen the formation of the Waitangi Tribunal, a select bicultural group of eminent citizens. Its task is to inquire into Maori grievances arising from perceived breaches of the Treaty. Such findings are then passed to the Government, together with suggested remedies where deemed justified.

Current TITLES

The twentieth century has seen many changes in the legal status of Maori land tenure, with titles now falling into different categories. Some are ordinary freehold titles. Others are held as various reserve lands, while some still remain as original 'Maori land'. This latter category, referred to as papatupu, is land which has never held a European title.

Tribal OWNERSHIP

Considerable areas are still controlled by tribes and subtribes. Legislation over the years has established a system of shareholding, providing an interest for all tribal members in certain blocks. Shares allocated to individuals have traditionally depended on the strength of that member's family at the time initial titles were awarded by the Maori Land Court. Today much tribal land, particularly where shareholdings have been amalgamated into corporations, is extremely productive in farming, horticulture and forestry. Other substantial holdings have been leased to private and public companies for similar schemes.

Today, land holdings are generally less important than income from employment as a means of supporting a family. However, it would be impossible to overestimate the importance of land to the Maori as a means of preserving national identity and mana.

Social order

Population growth and permanent (or semi-permanent) settlements brought a need for a clearly defined social system.

Tribal HIERARCHY

Within the iwi (total tribe), hapu (sub-tribe) or even whanau (family), leadership and authority lay initially with the senior male line. Tradition dictated that the first-born son of a chief (already established by inheritance) would succeed to that rank as would his own first-born in due course and so on. A first-born female could not normally succeed to a leadership role (although this did happen on rare occasions) but would nevertheless hold considerable rank and prestige.

Paratene Maioha, a chief of Waingaroa.

If a first-born male proved an inadequate leader he would still hold acknowledged seniority, but the tasks of leadership and tribal administration might then fall to a more capable younger brother. In fact, this provision extended even further so that a person holding no inherited chiefly rank might, through sheer ability, attain an elevated status within the tribe for himself and his descendants.

Status and POWER

Places in society were largely predetermined by ancestry and recognised generally as falling into two categories. There were the rangatira (those of superior or aristocratic class) and the ware or tutua (those thought of as commoners).

Within the rangatira ranks the term 'ariki' denoted the senior son of the tribe's senior family, acknowledging him as the tribal leader. He had the power, after consultation, to rule and direct his people, particularly in matters of warfare and politics. A further group of rangatira rank were the tohunga (priests), who specialised mainly in religious matters. A presumed ability of some to communicate with the gods and to work both beneficial and evil spells made them probably the most important (or feared) of all leaders. Other rangatira concerned themselves with more practical matters and were known as experts in the arts of agriculture, fishing, canoe or house building, carving, and so on.

Te Ohu, a tohunga of the Ngati Maniapoto.

At the bottom of society was the taurekareka (slave), usually a captive taken during a successful military campaign.

GENEALOGY

Each family group preserved and proclaimed its association with other groups by means of extensive genealogies (whaka-papa). Experts in this field were well able to quote genealogies not only for family relationships, but also of associated tribes and subtribes. This often involved citing ancestry extending far beyond the period of settlement in New Zealand. Even today, at functions where strict Maori protocol is observed, expert speakers will quote extensive genealogies to indicate their own and other relationships to the assembly.

Tribal NAMES

Throughout New Zealand, tribal names usually commemorate revered or founding ancestors, and most carry the prefix ngati, ngai or ati. In the Rotorua district, for instance, we find Ngati Whakaue (the people or descendants of the chief Whakaue); Ngati Pikiao (the people of the chief Pikiao) and so on. These two subtribes and their many other related groups form part of an iwi (a major tribe) known collectively as Te Arawa. This was the name of the canoe which originally brought them to New Zealand.

The family

The whanau (family unit) was the most vital aspect of Maori society. However the term 'whanau' embraced a much wider group than 'family' implies to Europeans. It included in-laws and all those associated by blood ties to a fairly remote degree. Individual and immediate family life separate from this wider group could hardly be said to exist.

POSSESSIONS

Dependence on the wider family group was influenced also by the collective ownership of vital assets such as favoured territories. Within these areas individual families generally occupied and worked certain acknowledged cultivations. Personal property was, as a rule, limited to a few garments, a few tools, weapons and perhaps a treasured ornament or two.

Puhi.

CONSULTATION

Though families controlled much of their day-to-day routine, anything of general consequence required public discussion. Matters of collective security or welfare demanded the attention of all. Family concerns, such as marriage or local disputes (at least within the more important ranks) were publicly debated.

Family NUMBERS

Continuity and increase in population were very important. Within the rangatira class, additional numbers ensured a continuation of that more exalted rank. The lesser echelons benefited from an increase in labour force. There was also the advantage of family members becoming numerous enough to establish their own hapu (subtribe). Their senior male members would then be elevated to rangatira class, at least in this new grouping. Procreation was therefore considered vital.

Sex and MARRIAGE

Matters of sex were discussed openly in Maori society. Sexual experience among the young was recognised as normal, and until adulthood brought little or no censure. There were, however, some prohibitions. Affairs between first cousins before marriage were frowned upon, though marriage between the same was not a rarity. As a general rule young people were free to choose their own mates but selection from within the same tribe was encouraged. Economic and political alliances sometimes dictated a marriage further afield.

Girls promised in infancy to the sons of important families were denied the freedom of love affairs in order to avoid the prospect of insulting a prospective husband. Daughters of a powerful chief might be forbidden sexual freedom until an alliance could be forged for her with a chief of similarly high rank. Such virgin chieftainesses were termed 'puhi' and would be watched over by attendants whose task was to protect them from temptation or unwanted suitors until marriage.

It is generally accepted that in Maori society girls reached maturity at a young age and would probably marry during their early or mid-teens. Childbirth was not unusual from the age of fifteen and by the mid-twenties perhaps four or five children might have been produced. Young men were generally at least twenty before taking a wife, and if she was sterile he could take an additional wife.

Marriage formalities played little part among commoners. Couples simply took up quarters together, an extended period of compatibility proclaiming them publicly to be man and wife. Among important ranks, however, there would be much inter-family discussion leading to a handing-over of the bride to the husband. A chief of rank generally took more than one wife.

Divorce or separation was common enough and there seems to have been no specific ritual involved. Estrangements generally arose through desertion by the husband rather than the wife. The physical or mental abuse of a wife of chiefly status or adultery was sometimes a reason for separation and often led to warfare. Where battles were avoided there were frequently reprisals against the relatives of the offender. Possessions, sometimes including land, would be demanded by, and paid to, those of the offended party.

Maori wedding, an adoption of European custom and dress.

31

The art of carving

Carving is believed by many to represent the ultimate indigenous art form of New Zealand and such work, when produced by acknowledged experts, involves more than mere decorative embellishments. Quality carvings pay deep respect to ancestors, history, myths and legends.

ORIGINS

Maori carvings are unlike most other carvings in Polynesia, yet there is a common thread in all Polynesian art that suggests development from a single original source. It seems likely that the basic patterns were brought here with the first migrants from the central Pacific area. Some experts suggest they had an even earlier and more distant origin, perhaps as far afield as Melanesia or even India.

The distinctive differences in New Zealand Maori carving owe much to the isolation of the Maori from the rest of Polynesia over many centuries. There were other factors too. An abundance of timber, such as the kauri and totara, provided a perfect medium for the art, and there was an ample supply of greenstone (jade) from which chisels of superb quality could be fashioned.

Traditional carving tools — stone adze and chisels.

A new ERA

The greatest advance for the art of the carver came with the introduction of steel tools in the late eighteenth and early nineteenth centuries. Few carvings as we know them today existed in the pre-European era. With the new-found equipment, richly carved houses, canoes, monuments to the dead and a multitude of other pieces became relatively common. The expert carvers rose to an even more exalted rank because of the increased demands, and they were eagerly sought after.

The human FIGURE

The dominant feature of Maori carving is the human figure, portrayed in varying form. The face, often with protruding tongue, appears both in full face and profile, the profile frequently distorted and referred to as 'manaia'. Not always easy to detect, the manaia motif, with its sometimes bird-like appearance, is said by some to indicate an original affinity with earlier Polynesian communities as far afield as Easter Island. The curves, loops, spirals and other geometric patterns are each of traditional form and individually named.

Today's carvers have greater freedom of expression through a wider range of commissions and new mediums such as compressed timber products.

A declining ART

The wars in New Zealand of the 1860s and subsequent rapid decline in Maori population brought in their wake an unproductive era, during which maintenance of carvings was much neglected. Once-beautiful works of art fell into disrepair and simply rotted away. The problem was compounded by collectors working on behalf of private buyers and overseas museums. Many of New Zealand's finer items, ranging from meeting houses to personal ornaments, were taken from the country.

REVIVAL

The twentieth century has seen a resurgence of the Maori population and enthusiasm for their endangered arts. Largely as a result of the establishment of the New Zealand Maori Arts and Crafts Institute at Te Whakarewarewa, Rotorua, a constant stream of qualified carvers, trained by master craftsmen, are emerging to carry their skills back to the people throughout the country.

The skills of the weaver

Of immediate concern to the Maori arriving in Aotearoa was bodily protection against the cold weather. Plaited textiles were generally stiff, rough and uncomfortable next to the skin. In response to this problem the Maori developed a weaving technique which made possible the production of garments which had no equal in Polynesia.

Above: Phormium tenax (New Zealand flax).

FLAX

It was the quality of the harakeke (New Zealand flax plant, *Phormium tenax*) and the superb thread produced from its fibrous leaves that supplied the raw material for these garments, of which the cloak became the most highly prized item. A superlative system of weaving, generally referred to as 'downward' or 'finger' weaving, was evolved which led to their production. Few items in New Zealand carry the prestige associated with the possession of one of these cloaks.

The body of each cloak is produced in much the same way. It is the outer decoration which identifies the particular style.

DECORATION

The korowai cloak is decorated with short, double lengths of twisted fibre, generally dyed black to contrast with the cream-coloured body of the garment. Perhaps the most important decoration on the korowai was a coloured taniko border, which added a bright geometric pattern of finely woven

Far left: Rolling fibre against the leg produced a thread of even form.

Left: A prepared hank of thread receives its 'softening up' treatment.

Above: Flax today serves for both traditional and contemporary items.

Above right: Korowai cloak and (below), piupiu skirt show the versatility of flax fibre.

special fibre. Other cloaks had short lengths of narrow-diameter rolls of the flax leaf attached to the woven fabric. These same rolls, when of full length and fastened close together on a plaited waistband, form the piupiu (skirt) worn by virtually all cultural parties today.

Though rarely seen now outside of museums, kahu kuri, or dogskin cloaks, were highly prized in former times. Vertical strips of the dog hide, usually in alternate colours, were sewn to the body of the cloak with the hairy surface showing. Of all cloaks, however, it is those adorned with feathers (kahu huruhuru) that were most sought after and retain a degree of influence found in few other possessions of the Maori.

The skills of taniko weaving are passed on by this old expert of earlier times.

Feathered CLOAKS

Feathers from a variety of birds were used in cloak making, and when feathers of one particular species such as the kiwi were employed exclusively, the cloak would be termed a 'kahu kiwi'. These kahu kiwi were, and still are, the most highly prized and are indicative of high rank. Because of the total protection of our native bird population today, feathers of imported exotic species are used in most modern cloaks.

Better quality garments were also a highly prized item of gift and exchange. Even today, the most valued gifts on ceremonial occasions are often finely woven and decorated cloaks.

Though the weaving of high quality garments fell to the lot of recognised experts, woven or plaited functional items were probably part of the almost daily routine of most women.

Though flax forms the basis for cloaks such as this, it is the distinctive and beautiful kiwi feather covering that sets such garments apart.

Jack Lang

Baskets & CONTAINERS

Kete (kits) were items in constant use and took many forms, utilising not only flax but also leaves of the ti kouka, or cabbage tree, and nikau palm. In past times kete were woven for specific purposes, and their size and shape reflected this. Today the most distinctive features of kete are the variety of styles that express the skills of the weaver.

A small flax platter or shallow kit known as rourou was probably the first item attempted by an aspiring weaver. Roughly woven from green flax and serving as both plate and container, they were generally discarded immediately after use. More elaborate and specialised baskets were constructed for extracting oil or juice from various forest berries, or for steeping others in water to remove certain poisonous constituents. Seed kumara for future planting was kept in a loosely woven kit known as toiki, often made from the finer vines of kakareao (supplejack). Another, termed 'patua', was not a woven kit but was made from the bark of the totara tree. Folded back upon itself and tied,

Kete

it would readily hold water.

Small finely woven bags (putea) were used for holding small articles. Many were woven from the leaves of pingao, a coastal plant, producing a rich golden colour when dried for use. Even smaller bags, delicately worked and containing fragrant moss or gum, were hung from a cord around the neck.

Kits and baskets are today the most commonly used of all indigenous products.

Floor MATS

The whariki, or floor mat, has always been an important part of the work of Maori weavers. They undoubtedly once provided protection against dust in dirt-floored houses. They were also utilised as coverings for the ferns and rushes used as bedding. Though carpets might now cover the floor of a meeting house there will still be a place for these traditional items. Such mats might, for instance, be laid beneath the mattress of an overnight visitor of distinction. They

A proud weaver sits in front of her newly produced whariki (c. 1900).

are also usually placed beneath a coffin during the tangihanga (mourning period preceding burial) as a particular mark of respect to the deceased. In a blending of Christianity with tradition, fine mats may be used for participants at a wedding ceremony to stand on. It was once not uncommon for the birth of an important child to take place on an especially fine mat, which was woven for the purpose.

Games and amusements

Traditional PURSUITS

Common sports such as running, jumping, a type of boxing and wrestling were regularly encouraged to build strength and endurance. Other more specialised games were designed to improve dexterity.

Spear-throwing, generally using toe-toe flower stalks, was a favourite pastime. A means of acquiring accuracy, this exercise involved two players throwing shafts at each other in turn, the skill of the non-thrower being displayed in his ability to dodge, deflect or catch the shaft thrown by the other. Ti rakau, another game, involved the tossing of short (though heavy) sticks, held vertically, among members of a group kneeling in a circle. The pace of the movements gradually quickened, the winner ultimately being the last to succeed in holding all catches. A similar game, ti ringa, was devised to sharpen eye and hand movements. It involved two individuals facing one another, one performing a series of hand movements, generally against the body, which the opposite player was expected to anticipate and duplicate instantly. Though a scoring system existed, the game's aim was to equip the players for the skilled use of hand-held weapons.

A native swing (moari), recorded by George French Angus.

HAKA

While not strictly speaking a game, the haka (posture dance) was, and still is, one of the most popular of all Maori amusements, requiring a considerable degree of manual dexterity. Energetic movements of hands, feet and body, glaring eyes and protruding tongue combined with emotionally charged word, bring a ready response and spirited participation from the audience.

Though now an inevitable part of every cultural group performance, the haka has a special significance within Maori

SPORT

Though traditional games and amusements are still avidly followed within Maori society, the same people play a vital role in national sports. New Zealand's famous rugby and rugby league teams (the All Blacks and Kiwis respectively) have always relied on the special skills and flair of their Maori members.

society. In former times, displeasure over perceived wrongs or grievances generally found expression in the form of a haka. Its performance might, however, also be used to recount great feats or to give a special welcome to an honoured guest. Women frequently participated.

Whipping tops, stilts, knucklebones, cat's cradle, kite flying, darts and swimming were other favourite pastimes.

POI

Of all dances, those featuring the poi are the most appreciated by New Zealanders and visitors alike. Originally about the size of an orange, the poi consisted of a finely woven flax net of close mesh stuffed usually with the down of the bullrush head, and so packed that it formed a near-perfect sphere. Various modern substitute materials are often used today. The dancer holds the poi by means of an attached cord, varying in length from about 20 cm to perhaps a metre.

In group performances the poi is generally held by a short cord and the dancers, always in perfect unison, twirl the poi outwards, upwards and over the shoulder, rapping it often against the other hand or body. Solo performers can use the long cord to manipulate up to four poi.

Above: Long poi

Above left: Ti rakau (stick game), here performed for an audience, was designed to develop speed and dexterity in hand movements.

Maori women have similarly participated fully as members of our world class Silver Ferns netball team. There would be few sports, if any, in which Maori are not involved at every level from national prominence to recreational enjoyment.

Education

Pre-European Maori education cannot be judged in terms of today's requirements. Though knowing nothing of the written word or of anything beyond their own world, they were, in the main, totally educated in all matters affecting their survival and pleasure in an often hostile environment.

As in almost all societies, education of the child began in the home. There was an advantage for the Maori in that communal living provided an immediate and extended family. A child was rarely without adult company. Though lifespans were short in pre-European days there were always 'the old', anxious to pass on their accumulated knowledge to succeeding generations.

SCHOOLING

Once childhood was over boys were required to assist in most of the general daytime manual tasks. Evenings, however, were spent with family members, listening to the history, traditions and myths of the tribe. They learned of family connections and genealogy, and took instruction in the elementary laws of tapu, those rules and restrictions governing conduct towards their environment, other people and the gods. Girls participated in most of these activities and were also instructed in the arts of weaving, the plaiting of mats and baskets, and the proper preparation of a wide variety of food-stuffs.

In addition, there was a general study of astronomy to determine the propitious days for fishing and hunting, or to calculate the correct periods for cultivation. All were taught to recognise the value of a multitude of different plants, the movement of birds and the times of spawning and migration of fish. Every boundary point of their land had to be known by heart, as did the name of each important or conspicuous headland, hill, ridge, stream, rock, spring, tree or bend of a river. A practical knowledge of these things represented 'education' in the fullest sense of the word for the times.

Spiritual LORE

Another branch of education dealt with the spiritual lore of the Maori, an aspect of their life governing almost every activity.

Instruction of this kind was provided by certain men skilled in tribal history, tradition, legend and ritual. Some specialised in one or more of these fields, the most noted (and feared) being those whose expertise related to sorcery. Most, if not all, were believed to possess the ability to communicate and intercede directly with the gods. These experts were referred to as tohunga (priest or expert) and tutored their pupils in the seclusion of a special house known as a whare wananga (house of learning). Pupils were drawn from the more illustrious families and faced rigorous tests to determine their suitability. Once accepted, they remained under severe restriction, often for long periods, because of the sacredness of the knowledge being absorbed. When ultimately qualified they joined the small but powerful group who largely determined the course of events for their people.

Sydney Yates conducts classes in the whare wananga at Ohinemutu, Rotorua.

A different WORLD

When Europeans arrived with an array of remarkable possessions, strange ways and Christianity, and the news that Aotearoa was but a tiny part of the universe, the world of the Maori was turned upside down. In the scramble to acquire these new goods, especially firearms and alcohol, concern for ancient lore and tradition began to crumble. A devastating decline in Maori population in the nineteenth century accelerated this loss of cultural heritage, which reached its lowest ebb during the final decades of the century. Fortunately some of the old experts survived, leading to a revival of cultural enthusiasm during the twentieth century.

In many Maori communities elders conduct classes in tribal lore, etiquette, genealogy, and so on. These subjects and arts such as carving and weaving are also taught at centres such as the New Zealand Maori Arts and Crafts Institute at Rotorua.

Education TODAY

The New Zealand national school syllabus has been the same for both Maori and non-Maori children by law since 1928. Now, however, in various parts of the country bicultural and in some places total 'Maori immersion' schools (kura kaupapa Maori) are being introduced in increasing numbers.

Though still too few, there are more Maori students reaching the highest levels of education. Maori men and women are eminent in all professions and play a key role among university academic staff. There are Maori schoolteachers at every level, many of them principals. In every field of endeavour the Maori is playing an increasing role.

Language

The indigenous language of New Zealand represents a very small but distinct part of the Austronesian family of languages. Once referred to as Malayo-Polynesian, these languages are found over a vast area of the world's surface, stretching from Madagascar in the west to Easter Island in the east. Within the Polynesian triangle they extend north/south from the Hawaiian Islands to New Zealand.

Samuel Marsden and Thomas Kendall arrive at the Bay of Islands in 1814. (Picturesque Atlas of Australasia, 1886.)

The eastern INFLUENCE

Within Polynesia, language experts define distinct eastern and western influences. In each of these spheres differences occur between the various island groups and even between some individual islands making up those groups. The Maori language falls within the area of eastern influence and seems to have derived from the language originally spoken by the inhabitants of the Society and Marquesas Islands. Despite this common origin with other eastern Pacific islands there are sufficient differences (because of long separation) to make communication between the various groups less than easy. Movement into the western sphere or beyond virtually rules out all oral communication.

41

Children at kohanga reo.

The written FORM

European knowledge of Pacific languages began during Captain Cook's second voyage here during 1772–75. The young naturalist George Forster, who accompanied Cook, collected a series of basic vocabularies. This was the earliest work on which the present classification of Pacific languages is based.

It was not until 1815 that the Maori language was put into written form by the missionary Thomas Kendall, who had arrived at the Bay of Islands a year earlier. By 1820 the Church Missionary Society had (with the help of Kendall) produced a grammar and vocabulary of 100 pages, the first serious study of the language.

New ENTHUSIASM

The last few decades of the twentieth century have seen a wave of enthusiasm for the promotion of the Maori language. Foremost in this respect are the Maori women whose efforts have seen the set-ting up of kohanga reo (language nests) where preschool children are introduced to the language. There is also a growing awareness of the value of bilingual primary schools so that the initial efforts of kohanga reo are not lost. At secondary school level, Maori language is generally offered as an optional subject, though this is not yet universal. Recent years have seen the emergence of largely privately funded schools where the entire teaching process (including the accepted national syllabus subjects) is conducted in the Maori language.

An official LANGUAGE

The Maori language is no longer commonly heard during ordinary day-to-day affairs except, perhaps, in a few isolated rural communities. However, it is invariably used during formal Maori functions where tribal protocol is observed. In addition, both Maori and English are recognised as official languages in New Zealand and either may be used when occasion demands.

Life and death

The Maori believed that life began with the primeval parents, Rangi (the sky father) and Papatuanuku (the earth mother), who lay together in a timeless embrace. To the pair were born a multitude of children, confined between the parents' bodies in total darkness. Eventually the children rebelled, forced the parents apart and emerged into the world of light. These children became the gods of the Polynesian world and included Tane, god of the forests. According to tradition it is only the strength of the great trees of Tane that keep the primeval pair apart. Should too many trees be lost we may again find ourselves confined to a world of darkness.

Love between Rangi and Papatuanuku has never ceased. The rain and dew that fall are the tears of Rangi, the sky father, while rising mists are a sign of unrequited love from Papatuanuku, the earth mother.

Human LIFE

These first gods were all men. It was Tane who first created woman by forming an image in human form from earth, part of the body of the earth mother. He breathed life into this form which sneezed, opened its eyes, breathed and became the first human female. She was named Hine-ahu-one. Tane took her as his wife and from that pair have descended the host of demi-gods of varying categories, and so on down to the Maori of today.

A young Maori mother carries her baby in a once commonplace and traditional manner — slung behind her in a blanket, c. 1914.

Each new BIRTH

The birth of children in pre-European times attracted little ceremony except within chiefly families. There was, however, a tapu or prohibition attached to all women before confinement. They were segregated from the community, generally in a special hut or shelter known as a whare kohanga (nest house). Here the expectant mother was attended by other women skilled in such matters. At times posts were set in the ground on which she could strain to assist delivery, which took place in a squatting position. A tohunga or priest would also attend and recite charms and sacred prayers to ensure a satisfactory birth.

Once the child was born, the umbilical cord was cut and tied by the tohunga who then took that and the placenta away, hiding them in some secret place. Finally all traces of tapu were removed from the mother and child, leaving them free to join the community.

The birth of important children, particularly a first-born male, brought much celebration during which gifts, including favoured foods, were made to the mother and child.

BAPTISM

A later baptism was of particular consequence. Holding the child in his arms, the tohunga would pray that the infant, if a male would become a renowned warrior. During the prayer the child was sprinkled with water from a sacred source and endowed at the same time with its chosen name.

Life's END

There was much ceremony when life came to an end. This event, perhaps more than any other, is still marked by close adherence to ancient tradition.

In former times men preferred to die in battle, in order to be remembered as a warrior. Death through sickness or accident was usually ascribed to some transgression of a tapu law or the malevolent efforts of an enemy.

If death was imminent, the dying person was removed to temporary quarters. This was to prevent the obligatory destruction or abandonment of a dwelling because of the potent tapu effect of a death occurring within. In addition, a chief would, if possible, be carried to the open marae to make his final public speech.

Cape Reinga, or Rerenga Wairua, the departure point for spirits on their long trip back to Hawaiki.

Frequently a dying person would request a favoured food, or water from some special source. Every effort was made to meet these wants, after which death came contentedly.

The moment of death was signalled by much wailing, crying and often, in later times, by the firing of guns. In pre-European times immediate steps were taken to prepare the corpse by trussing it, drawing the knees up to the chest. The body was covered with fine garments, the hair was oiled and combed then adorned with precious feathers. This practice was gradually replaced by the conventional use of coffins.

The TANGIHANGA

Tribal customs vary but generally the open coffin lies within the porch of a meeting house or an adjacent shelter. Fine mats and precious heirlooms cover the body and (since the introduction of photography) portraits of relatives are placed nearby. Women of the immediate and extended family maintain a vigil beside the coffin during the mourning period, known as the tangihanga. This once lasted as long as was necessary for relatives and friends to visit and pay their last respects. In the days before modern transport this might mean ten days or more. The law now determines the maximum time a body may remain unburied.

The final JOURNEY

Souls of the departed are believed to hover above their loved ones for a time. They then leave on a final journey back to Hawaiki, the original homeland of all Polynesians. The initial flight is to the northern point of New Zealand, now called Cape Reinga. To the Maori it is

Alexander Turnbull Library

Top: A tangi at Tarewa, Rotorua.

Bottom: Visitors from Parihaka advance onto a Taranaki marae for a tangi, preceded by their own marae flag.

Rerenga Wairua, the departure place of spirits. Here the soul paused, looked back with affection, climbed down from the rocky promontory to the beach below then returned to the spirit world.

BURIAL

In former times the deceased was generally buried in the earth, but was sometimes suspended in a tree or placed in a temporary tomb. Later, the remains were recovered, the bones cleaned and wrapped in bundles, and then deposited in various secret locations. This was to prevent any desecration by an enemy.

Warfare and weapons

Warfare was an ever-present part of life for the Maori. No able-bodied male was exempt from service and it was not rare for women to participate or at least accompany their menfolk on expeditions.

Battles occurred largely as a result of insults against a tribal group or one of its important members. Such insults had to be avenged, and were often used as an excuse to acquire another's land. As each group felt it a point of honour to respond in kind to any attack, an initial minor affray might easily escalate into a major conflict.

In pre-European times warfare was probably less disastrous than traditions indicate. Hand-to-hand conflict with original weapons did at times result in severe casualties but it was the arrival of the musket that ushered in a devastating period for the Maori.

Wherever pre-European populations gathered, nearby hilltops became fortified sites, protecting local residents against aggression.

Masters of STRATEGY

Face-to-face battles between warring groups were commonplace but the Maori was, in fact, a master of strategy. Wherever possible, unexpected manoeuvres, decoys, ambush or subterfuge were used to gain ascendancy over an enemy. Instances of single combat between opposing chiefs to determine an outcome were rare.

46

The victorious were rarely generous and those of the vanquished unable to escape were usually killed unless spared to become slaves. As an added insult casualties were generally eaten, the heads of important victims being preserved as trophies.

Above from left to right: Short club – kotiate, long club – tewhatewha, short club – wahaika, long club – taiaha.

DEFENCES

Because of the almost constant threat of attack, the Maori were obliged to provide a safe retreat wherever they congregated. In former heavily populated areas the hilltops are still scarred with remnants of once-fortified sites. Known as pa, these strongholds employed deep surrounding trenches, terraces and palisades (sometimes one or all) for defence. Though the value of the pa as a refuge declined with the introduction of muskets and artillery, Maori 'engineers' were quick to devise sites to cope with the new threat.

WEAPONS

Pre-European warfare was almost entirely a hand-to-hand affair. Projectiles played very little part. Spears varying in length from two to three metres and even longer were sometimes used as such, but were generally for thrusting between palisades of a pa.

Most other weapons were clubs, the long ones known as taiaha, pouwhenua and tewhatewha. These averaged about 1.5 m in length and were made of a tough wood. One end was flattened into a blade for striking (as with the quarterstaff) while the other was pointed for stabbing.

As well as this long weapon, a patu (short club) was usually carried. Made of wood, bone or stone (the most prized being greenstone) it was stuck in the warrior's thickly woven war

PUHARA. WHAKAREWAREWA.

Above: Toki pou tangata (ceremonial adze) with greenstone blade.

Opposite: Maori soldiers aboard the Aquitania *during the Second World War.*

belt. Known as mere, kotiate and wahaika (depending on design), each had a wide, flat blade, the extremity ground to a sharp edge. A thrusting rather than a striking weapon, the patu's sharp front edge was brought against an opponent's temple or neck, a final blow being delivered to the skull as the enemy fell.

The MUSKET

The most disastrous period of Maori warfare came with the introduction of European muskets. Those living in the Bay of Islands area were the first to acquire these in significant numbers. As a result they exacted heavy retribution on neighbouring tribes in order to settle ancient scores. They then began a series of expeditions south with devastating effect. Missionaries of the time estimated that in the twenty years before 1849 some 80,000 people died in the intense intertribal warfare involving the musket.

Maori/European WARFARE

The nineteenth century saw two periods of warfare between European and Maori. The first occurred in the Bay of Islands where the earliest (and at the time the only) important European settlement, Kororareka, was sited.

For the Maori there was discontent over the loss of land, a loss of income from a declining whaling industry, the imposition of government taxes and finally the removal of the seat of government to Auckland. In January 1845 the chief Hone Heke and supporters cut down the flagstaff and sacked Kororareka to show their rejection of British authority. Several severe engagements between government troops and Maori forces followed, a battle in January 1846 bringing hostilities to a close.

A much larger conflict broke out in the 1860s and early 1870s. Continuing ignorance of Maori land tenure, political pressures and demands for land from European settlers had brought deep resentments. Promises made to the Maori under the terms of the Treaty of Waitangi were circumvented and in February 1860 there was war in Taranaki. By July 1863 the conflict had spread to the Waikato district and a year later the Bay of Plenty was embroiled. Eventually warfare spread throughout the central North Island.

A new and violent phase erupted between 1868 and 1872 with the emergence of Te Kooti Rikirangi and his anti-British-settler army. His four-year campaign was ultimately halted in 1872, bringing a disastrous decade to a close.

Though all warfare within New Zealand ended during the late nineteenth century, Maori have continued to provide a remarkable record of fighting qualities since that time. Participating always as volunteers, they have served overseas with distinction alongside Pakeha New Zealanders throughout the twentieth century.

Young men from virtually every tribal area fought with valour during the Boer War in Africa. Their heroism was renowned as they battled at Gallipoli and in France during the First World War. The exploits of the 28th Maori Battalion during the Second World War are legendary and have left an imperishable record matched by few, if any, units anywhere. Since then, Maori have served in every theatre of war where New Zealand troops have been involved, and they continue to be a vital element within our armed forces.

Harris Album

49

Population

It is not known how many Polynesians arrived in Aotearoa in the first major migration nor how many subsequent immigrants there were, if any, in those distant times. Tradition speaks of separate arrivals but they would have been few.

Though both the North and South Islands have been inhabited for a similar period, perhaps no more than 10 to 15 percent of the population were living south of the central North Island when Europeans first arrived.

First ESTIMATES

Estimates of the immediate pre-European Maori population vary considerably. Captain Cook provided an estimate of 100,000 in 1773 but this could only have been a guess. Similar numbers have since been suggested by archaeologists based on pa-site numbers and available food resources. General opinion among experts puts the figure at somewhere between 125,000 and 150,000. Given a settlement of perhaps 900 years before 1773, an initial group of about fifty people of both sexes

This woman, calloused, crippled and blind, appears to have survived many bouts of illness and disease.

could conveniently reach numbers in excess of 100,000 during that period.

A drastic DECLINE

By 1840 the Maori population had dropped to some 80,000 to 90,000. Firearms, alcohol and disease introduced during the largely lawless heydays of sealing and whaling (c.1795–1830) were mainly responsible. Diseases against which the Maori had no immunity decimated numbers even in remote areas. The musket brought a devastating era of intertribal warfare while an excess of alcohol hastened the decline.

Epidemics continued through the middle 1800s. Influenza, measles, whooping cough, typhoid, tuberculosis and other illnesses ran their course. These, combined with a collapse of morale over the loss of lands and warfare with the British military, reduced the population to its lowest ebb of 43,000 in 1896.

RECOVERY

The twentieth century has seen a constant increase in the Maori population. The most spectacular era was between 1926 and 1961 when it leapt from some 70,000 to more than 167,000. Today the total is almost twice that number. Very few of this group, however, are of pure Maori descent. The total includes all who care to declare themselves Maori, regardless of the extent of their Maori ancestry. Under some circumstances proof of ancestry may be required.

Health

Conditions in New Zealand for the first arrivals were adequate for a healthy lifestyle. Those surviving childhood could expect to reach an adult age of perhaps 30 years. Life expectancy varied between the mid-twenties and early thirties. Those 40 or over would be considered very old.

Infant MORTALITY

Childbearing was a hazardous event. The average woman could expect (from her late-teen years) to produce perhaps five children with a three- or four-year interval between births. Infant mortality may have been as high as 25 percent so most mothers would see at least one of their children die in infancy. Because the mother's own lifespan was short, the extended family system was essential to ensure the welfare of at least the younger children.

ADULTHOOD

Hard physical work came with adulthood. This generally brought a degeneration of the joints and particularly the spine for both sexes. Beginning during the early twenties, such problems quickly progressed, bringing incapacity. A further problem (though not universal) was tooth wear. In some communities this was extreme, leading to an almost total tooth loss among the old, followed by malnutrition, disease and death. This affliction prevailed where fibrous or gritty products, such as fern root and dried seafoods, were commonplace.

Nothing is known of contagious diseases before the arrival of Europeans. However, they were unlikely because of the small population and isolated communities. As a result, Maori developed no natural immunities and subsequently faced devastating epidemics with the arrival of Europeans.

Causes and CURES

In early Maori society sickness was attributed to the patient offending the gods by breaching a tapu rule, or to sorcery by an enemy. A tohunga would define the transgression and intercede on the patient's behalf with the gods, or prescribe countermeasures if sorcery was suspected. A fatalistic belief that illness was a divine punishment left many of the sick with little will to survive. A very few plant remedies and some physical treatments were administered for minor ailments but only after the arrival of the European was there a systematic study of local herbs and plants.

Health PROBLEMS

Today's young and expanding Maori population is more than 320,000. Despite this, deaths from most of the common, potentially fatal diseases are still appreciably higher in the Maori than in the non-Maori. There has been a distinct reduction in the death rates for Maori children but for those over the age of 35 there is little improvement. Asthma, heart disease, diabetes, chronic respiratory and renal diseases and cancers cause a disproportionate number of deaths. Adult Maori females have the world's highest death rate from lung cancer.

New initiatives to combat these problems include a recognition of some traditional Maori medicines, an increase in Maori health workers, an awareness in hospitals of Maori cultural needs, and the introduction of community health programmes run by and for Maori people.

A father gives his son a cooling dip in the Wairoa River.

Keith McNabb

Music

Music plays a vital role in Maori life. It is a natural inheritance of Polynesian children who, from infancy, display a perfection of rhythm and measured time. No Maori function is complete without music, and song on these occasions is universal.

Left: In time to a rhythm provided by the group on the left, a line of workers begins the task of cultivation in unison.

The use of SONG

A multitude of songs, or waiata, have been composed over the centuries. They recount the history, myths and singular events of a people. Many reflect the composer's own emotions including hatred, contempt, grief, happiness and love. They have been composed to greet visitors, to appeal for help, and as an aid to heavy labour requiring collective effort. Songs were (and still are) a vital accompaniment to posture and other dances. An orator frequently breaks into song to emphasise a point and, joined by associates, concludes with another.

Songs were part of early ritual and essential to the repertoire of those conducting ceremonial matters. However, ancient songs contain so many allusions to obscure rites, myths, beliefs and incidents from the past that a vast knowledge of tribal lore is necessary for their understanding.

A different RANGE

Though often likened by non-Maori to religious chants, and

based on a different scale from western music, all Maori waiata possess distinct and individual airs. Within the range of those sounds used there are modulations and nuances appreciated only by the practised ear. These, with certain emphases and expressions, delight the initiated.

The Maori has readily adopted a western system for much of today's music but the waiata prevails on truly cultural occasions.

Musical
INSTRUMENTS

It was very largely wind instruments that provided music for the Maori.

Those thought of as trumpets were pu tatara and pu kaea. The pu tatara was made from the triton shell, to which a carved wooden mouthpiece was attached at the severed apex. It produced a loud call, frequently used to summon people together. The pu kaea was made of two hollowed wooden pieces bound together. In length it varied from about 60 cm to sometimes 200 cm. It was capable of producing a remarkably loud call.

Instruments resembling the flute are named putorino, whio, koauau and nguru. Wood or bone were the main materials used. The putorino was made of a hard wood in two hollowed-out pieces fitted together. Sound was emitted through a single opening on the upper surface, usually depicted as the mouth of a decorative carved face. The whio was similarly made but had four stops and was played flute-like by blowing across the upper end.

The koauau was a shortened form of whio, generally made of wood or bone. The preferred material was a short length of human bone obtained from a

slain enemy, adding much to the instrument's value. Bone was said to produce a sweeter sound than wood. The nguru, a curiously shaped short instrument, had an open lower end and an upper curved to a narrow aperture. Two and sometimes three stops were pierced on the upper surface, providing a varying pitch to the instrument's sharp clear whistle.

All these instruments varied greatly in size and shape so undoubtedly had little uniformity of pitch. Nevertheless, expert players received great acclaim, their skills still spoken of in tradition and legend.

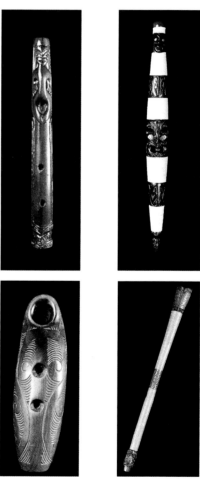

Maori musical instruments (*clockwise from top left*): *Koauau, putorino, nguru, pu kaea.*

54

Adornments and art

Perhaps the most remarkable adornment of the Maori was the full moko (facial tattoo) of chiefs. Often taking years to complete, it was literally 'carving in the flesh'. Having traced the outline with charcoal, the tohunga ta moko, or expert, began work. A narrow chisel, usually of finely honed albatross bone and hafted as an adze, was placed on the marked design and struck with a light mallet to make a groove. This was followed by a toothed chisel dipped in pigment. In this way the pigment was left within the incision made into the flesh. This process was continued but because of pain, severe swelling and inflammation, the many sessions required were each of short duration. The buttocks and thighs of some men were similarly treated. Women were also tattooed but generally only on the lips and chin. The main ingredient of the pigments was soot from the burnt resinous heartwood of kahikatea or burnt kauri gum.

This warrior shows the facial tattoo (moko) and puhoro on the thighs.

Dressing the HEAD

In common with Polynesian custom men wore their hair long, arranging it on the head as a top-knot. On occasions, feathers were stuck there, those of the huia, albatross and heron being most favoured. Combs of beautiful design in both wood and bone were also prized adornments. Though not always the case, women especially cut their hair short, or comparatively so. They also wore fewer items of personal adornment than men.

Ear pendants came in many forms. Clumps of feathers, often the soft white down of the albatross or gannet, were suspended from or through the lobe. Also prized was the triangular tooth of the mako shark. However, the most highly valued items were made of greenstone.

PENDANTS

The most used and prized material for ornaments was always greenstone.

These took various forms such as tiki, pekapeka, matau, koropepe, and kaka poria. Some designs undoubtedly derive from earlier woodcarving while others represent stylised objects such as the fish hook. Archaic forms of pendants made from sperm-whale teeth, moa bone and stone also existed but were rarely seen by the end of the eighteenth century. The prefix 'hei', for example in 'hei tiki', indicates the ornament was suspended from the neck.

TIKI

Of all ornaments, the tiki is most widely known. Of grotesque human form, it was eagerly sought by early collectors and so most were produced in post-European times. The predominant shape — tapering towards the sideways-tilted head — is considered the result of converting smaller greenstone adzes into tiki, once steel made stone adzes obsolete. A common perception that the tiki represents the human foetus and promoted fertility is dismissed by experts.

Rock ART

A great many rock drawings and paintings are found in certain areas of the South Island. Generally on the walls of rock shelters, they display a variety of forms. Many are clearly recognisable while others defy interpretation. The dissimilarity of these forms to Maori art at the time of European contact indicates early origins. They probably predate the fifteenth century.

The North Island has comparatively few examples of rock art. They differ from those of the South Island and also from each other. More akin to classic Maori art, they feature carvings rather than paintings.

Right: Pare Watene (top) and Taraia (below), wearing ornaments typical of rangatira.

56

The MEDIUM

Red ochre (kokowai) — burnt, powdered, then mixed with shark oil — provided the predominant red paint. Soot, prepared in the same way, gave black, while powdered white clay was sometimes similarly prepared. Valued for their protective qualities on timber, these original paints also made possible a distinctive form of Maori art. This was the decorative patterning applied to rafters inside superior houses. The introduction of European paints brought a proliferation of colour and in time led to some changes of original motifs and design.

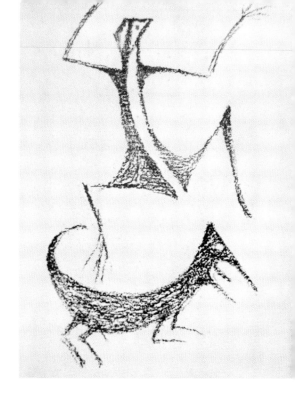

Right: Archaic petroglyphs or rock art.

Terence Barrow

A detail of a frontal post of the Te Hauke meeting house. This green-painted lizard is set between the legs of the ancestor depicted in the carving.

Gourd vessel with incised koru patterns. The rinds of gourds were cut into a variety of shapes, including horizontal bowls, food pots and water-bottles.

Neck ornaments called hei tiki were worn suspended on a plaited flax fibre cord. Made from greenstone, hei tiki are treasured as heirlooms.

Religion

Maori religion had its roots in the worship of nature and the veneration of ancestors. There was belief in an original supreme being known as Io. So sacred was this deity that the very name could only be uttered by important tohunga. From Io, in genealogical sequence, followed those named phases that ultimately brought light from darkness. Then came the evolution of man through a succession of gods and demi-gods. Eventually there was Tane, who created the first human woman. In some traditions Tane is synonymous with Tiki, regarded as the first human male.

A multitude of deities were individually responsible for every activity and concern of Maori society. Ritual was essential to ensure approval from the gods, with whom the tohunga kept constantly in touch. Governing all these supernatural matters were the laws of tapu.

TAPU

The most potent force in Maori life was tapu. Sometimes translated as 'sacred', its rules imposed a range of prohibitions intruding into almost every facet of life. No individual was exempt and any breach invited dire punishment from the gods. Serious transgressions could mean death. So strong was the belief in, and fear of, tapu that anything causing discomfort or worse was attributed to some breach of those laws. The only

Pre-European religion involved representations of certain gods, as in this stone figure on Mokoia Island (above) and sacred altars (top of opposite page).

Well hidden away were tiny storehouses carved into the rock. Here sacred offerings were made to the gods.

recourse was intercession with the gods by a tohunga on behalf of the offender.

Reasons for some tapu prohibitions are now obscure. Others were clearly imposed to benefit all. They included the conservation of habitat, food resources and wildlife as well as matters of health and behaviour.

Despite the wide acceptance of Christianity among the Maori of today, numerous aspects of original tapu observances persist. They are particularly noticeable with matters relating to sickness, death, burial and burying places. They are also evident in marae procedure and within the meeting house. In addition, experts on Maori lore are still consulted by some on matters of personal concern, especially those which seem to defy normal explanation. Many of New Zealand's non-Maori population have come to recognise and observe those remaining restrictions.

The MISSIONARIES

With missionaries came Christianity and rapid change for the Maori. Converts were persuaded to give up warfare, killing and cannibalism. Chiefs became monogamous, freed their slaves and renounced age-old claims for revenge. But allied to this was the collapse of their traditional religion which had for centuries provided a form of law and unity. Chiefs no longer commanded authority. Tapu restrictions were abandoned together with discipline. A social system built up over the centuries was rapidly disappearing and the new one being introduced by the Pakeha offered no real place for the Maori within its structure.

New RELIGIONS

The 1860s saw a new Maori religion known as Ringatu (upraised hand) established by the talented Maori zealot, Te Kooti Rikirangi. He had been unjustly imprisoned on the Chatham Islands in 1866. A Maori variant of Christianity, his faith also possessed elements of an earlier anti-British cult known as Hauhau.

Escaping to the mainland in 1868, Te Kooti and his supporters embarked on a violent campaign against settlers and government troops alike. Despite Te Kooti's death in 1893 the Ringatu religion, though small in terms of followers, exists today and is recognised officially.

A second religion of consequence was founded during the early 1920s by Tahupotiki Ratana. A once-obscure farmer, Ratana achieved national attention as a gifted faith healer. People flocked to his home and miraculous cures were attributed to him. He founded the Ratana Church and preached belief in God and the rejection of Maori tohungaism. Ratana died in 1939 but the church is still well supported and represented today in most Maori communities.

The Church of England, the Roman Catholic and Ratana faiths can today claim almost two-thirds of all Maori church members. Church of England adherents comprise perhaps half of this group.

Left: Ratana Church.

Above: Christian church interior, St Faith's, Ohinemutu, showing uniquely Maori motifs.

Politics

The first attempts to establish an effective Maori political group came with anti-land-selling leagues during the 1840s. Though extending into the 1850s they were relatively ineffective, due largely to ancient tribal animosities and well-funded government land purchase officers.

King MOVEMENT

In 1859 a further effort to unite the Maori resulted in the election of a Maori King. The aim was to promote a more united focus for Maori political views, and replace the decaying system of tribal authority. Despite the King Movement's intention to participate within the established system, it was ignored by the authorities. Denied any consultation on matters of Maori concern, it became a focus for Maori nationalism. That the Government chose to ignore it angered its supporters and further polarised Maori and settler.

The King Movement was more influential than the European community believed. Its opposition to land sales was viewed as a barrier to European expansion and a challenge to the Government. Attitudes hardened and increasingly hostile land disputes led to the wars of the 1860s which brought heavy losses to supporters of King Potatau, very largely the Waikato tribes. Much of their finest land was confiscated. Those affected withdrew into what became known as the King Country, and for twenty years prevented virtually any European penetration there.

The King Movement, however, survived, the leadership passing to succeeding generations of the first King's family.

The Maori QUEEN

With the death in 1966 of Koroki (the fifth Maori King) there was a significant change when, for the first time, a Maori Queen took the leading role.

At the time of King Koroki's death a gathering of non-Waikato tribal chiefs (as tradition dictated) decided that his

Tawhiao, the second Maori King.
(Picturesque Atlas of Australasia, 1886.)

Turangawaewae Marae, Ngaruawahia. Here Sir Kingi Ihaka addresses a group of Indian visitors. Queen Te Atairangikaahu stands behind him, dressed in black.

daughter, Princess Piki, should be the next ruler. The title of Queen was instituted but instead of using her own name, Princess Piki adopted that of her deceased mother and became Queen Te Atairangikaahu.

Though less political today than in earlier times, the King Movement, particularly during the reign of the Queen, has served as an even stronger rallying point for Maori sentiment. Based at Turangawaewae Marae at Ngaruawahia, the royal establishment has enhanced tremendously the prestige and mana of Maori people. Great respect for the Queen is universal in both the Maori and non-Maori population of New Zealand.

Maori REPRESENTATION

The Maori Representation Act of 1867 provided four specific seats in Parliament for the Maori people. Those appointed, however, were drawn only from chiefs who had supported the Government during the wars, or whose tribes had not been disaffected. The situation changed before the turn of the century. Though still restricted to four seats, members were solely elected by Maori adults of voting age. In addition, there has never been any legal barrier to the election of a Maori representative to general seats.

Maori INITIATIVES

In the early 1890s the wider Maori population made further attempts to unite all tribes and elect a Maori parliament named Kotahitanga (Oneness). This, they hoped, would allow them some form of self-government, independent of the New Zealand cabinet and Parliament. The objectives of Kotahitanga were to frame its own laws relating to Maori welfare and land matters. Despite meetings held over several years it failed to develop further largely because of disputes over leadership.

The Young Maori PARTY

During the 1890s a group of young, well-educated Maori men formed the Young Maori Party. Believing that Maori land should be retained and developed by their own people, they also demanded a stronger Maori voice in parliamentary affairs. The party was formally constituted in 1909 but soon after that its most influential leaders joined the existing Reform and Liberal parties. This led to the demise of the party. However, three of those leaders — Apirana Ngata, Maui Pomare and Te Rangi Hiroa (Peter Buck) — ultimately held parliamentary office and achieved more for their people during their terms than had ever been accomplished before. Each, in time, was knighted.

Twentieth century MOVES

Further Maori political parties followed during the 1920s. Muru Raupatu, Mana Maori Motuhake, and the Ratana Independent Movement were three. Of these only the Ratana group achieved any significant power. Ratana members first contested parliamentary seats in 1928 but by 1935 had formed an alliance with the New Zealand Labour Party. Since that time Maori parliamentary representatives for the four Maori seats have been almost totally allied to the Labour Party.

The Young Maori Party

Top: Sir Peter H. Buck (Te Rangi Hiroa), distinguished doctor, parliamentarian and anthropologist.

Middle: The Hon. Sir Maui Pomare, distinguished Maori leader, pioneer doctor among the Maori and Member of Parliament.

Bottom: The Hon. Sir Apirana Ngata, MA, LLB. Ngata was the first Maori graduate of the University of New Zealand, and a Member of Parliament from 1905 to 1943, attaining senior cabinet rank. He was a pioneer and advocate of Maori land development.

A new SYSTEM

With the introduction of a Mixed Member Proportional (MMP) system of government in 1996, Maori representation in parliament has been considerably strengthened. Distinct Maori seats are now settled at five, but this number will eventually increase in proportion to an ultimately larger Maori electoral roll. In the meantime the total number of Maori members of parliament has risen considerably with representatives in each of the four main political parties, some of whom hold ministerial portfolios. New Zealand First, in particular, has a large proportion of Maori MPs.

Dr the Hon. Peter Tapsell was the first Maori ever appointed Speaker of the House of Representatives.

Don Stafford's lifelong interest has led him to write much concerning the original Polynesian people of New Zealand.

His first major work was *Te Arawa* (1967), a substantial history of the Maori people of the Rotorua region, for which he was awarded the Elsdon Best Memorial Medal by the Polynesian Society.

He was commissioned in 1982 to compile the history of Rotorua for the Rotorua District Council, a role which involved almost six years of research, writing and the attendant tasks of book publication. That work resulted in *The Founding Years in Rotorua* (1986) and *The New Century in Rotorua* (1988). In 1994 the first volume of *Landmarks of Te Arawa* was published, followed in 1996 by the second, concluding volume. His other books include *Te Arawa Maori Trust Board* (1974), *The Romantic Past of Rotorua* (1977), *Rotorua 1880-1980* (1980) and *Flying the Thermal Skies* (1983).

Don Stafford has also published numerous articles and lectured widely within New Zealand and overseas. In 1980 he was awarded the MBE for his public services. A CBE followed in 1994 and an honorary doctorate from the University of Waikato.